AUG 3 1 2005

BEYOND THE GRAVE

by Judith Herbst

Ŀ Lerner Publications Company • Minneapolis

Lerner Publications Company
A division of Lerner Publishing Group
241 First Avenue North
Minneapolis, MN 55401 U.S.A.

Website address: www.lernerbooks.com

Library of Congress Cataloging-in-Publication Data

Herbst, Judith.
        Beyond the grave / by Judith Herbst.
            p.   cm. — (The unexplained)
        Includes index.
            ISBN: 0–8225–1627–6 (lib. bdg. : alk. paper)
        1. Parapsychology   I. Title. II. Series: Unexplained (Lerner Publications Company)
        BF.1031.H47 2005
        130—dc22   2004004511

Manufactured in the United States of America
1 2 3 4 5 6 – JR – 10 09 08 07 06 05

Table of Contents

The boundaries which divide Life from Death are at best shadowy and vague. Who shall say where the one ends, and the other begins?

—Edgar Allan Poe, "The Premature Burial"

CHAPTER 1
SPONTANEOUS HUMAN COMBUSTION *OR* HOW to Cook the TRUTH

There was nothing very spectacular about 67-year-old Mary Reeser except the way she died. On the night of July 1, 1951, she burst into flames in her Saint Petersburg, Florida, apartment. Nobody actually saw it happen, but that's the story that's been told and retold—and no doubt, altered—for over 50 years. But in case you haven't heard it, here it is.

The fiery death of Mary Reeser is thought by some to have been the result of spontaneous human combustion.

Oh ... and here's your grain of salt. You're going to need it.

Mary Reeser was not what you would call a party girl. By nine o'clock, she had already taken her sleeping pill, donned her nightie and satin slippers, and was ready to hit the sack. She settled into an armchair for one last smoke (and we do mean last) and a bit of musing over the day's events. Sometime between that cigarette and the arrival of a Western Union messenger the following morning, Mrs. Reeser's body burned, leaving behind only a piece of her spine, a charred liver, one foot, and her shrunken head. The carpet fared much better. It was only singed.

You don't have to be an arsonist or a firefighter to know that this is highly unlikely. If Mrs. Reeser goes up, so should the carpet, the furniture, and a good chunk of the apartment building. She had not simply

Investigators sort through the ashes in Mary Reeser's Saint Petersburg, Florida, home.

died of massive burns. She had been incinerated. This requires a temperature somewhere in the neighborhood of 1500°F. And don't kid yourself. It takes a while. Mrs. Reeser had to burn for several hours before she could be reduced to a pile of ash. Surely in that time, she would have at least set the curtains on fire. (In all fairness, we should mention that the armchair was cooked rather thoroughly.)

Did someone with a blowtorch or portable crematorium sneak up on Mrs. Reeser while she lay in a drug-induced sleep and blast away? Was Mrs. Reeser's lit cigarette the culprit? Or did the poor woman, as many have insisted, begin burning spontaneously?

Spontaneous human combustion (SHC for short) is said to occur when a person suddenly bursts into flames even though there is no source of ignition, such as a match. The heat is supposedly so intense that the person is almost completely consumed "within seconds." Sometimes a shrunken skull or part of a leg remains, and there may be a fatty residue, like the grease left after frying bacon. SHC is gruesome and frightening, the stuff of which nightmares are made, but is it real?

>> Hot Stories

Spontaneous human combustion has apparently been around for a while. In his novel *Bleak House,* published in 1853, Charles Dickens goes into great grisly detail when describing the fiery demise of a rag-and-bottle seller named Krook. The episode was fiction, of course, but Dickens based it on something he'd at least heard about. Supposedly, the Contessa Cornelia di Bandi had burst into flames in the 1700s, and her

This illustration by Halbot Browne in Charles Dickens's *Bleak House* depicts Krook's death by SHC.

All that remained of Dr. John Bentley after his death by fire was the lower half of his right leg.

terrible misadventure became the talk of Europe. The contessa's recognizable remains consisted of two legs (with stockings) and a partially burned head. In 1851 a Paris house painter was rumored to have gone up in flames after boasting that he could eat a lit candle. (Serves him right. How stupid is that?) The first bite started him off, and in about half an hour, his head and chest were toast. And John Bentley, a 90-year-old retired doctor, reportedly combusted spontaneously in the bathroom of his Pennsylvania home on December 5, 1966. Dr. Bentley left behind only his lower right leg, still clad in its bedroom slipper, and his walker, which strangely enough suffered little damage. The hideous picture seems to tell the story . . . but maybe not the whole story.

Finally, there is the Phyllis Newcombe story, which first turned up in the May 1942 edition of the science fiction magazine *Tomorrow*. That in itself should make you raise an eyebrow or two. Eight years later, *Fate* magazine published (almost) the same tale, and five years after that, a third version. In 1957 Eric Frank Russell, author of the first article, returned with a newer and considerably snappier account in his book *Great World Mysteries*. Using that as source material, Allan Eckart then went ahead and wrote his take on the Phyllis Newcombe story. By 1964 the truth had been effectively buried under a tangle of rewrites and editorial flights of fancy. Here's the essence of all the rewrites.

One evening, smack in the middle of a crowded dance floor at a ballroom somewhere in England, a young woman suddenly burst into flames and was reduced to ash in a matter of minutes. Her fiancé tried in vain to extinguish the fire, which was so intense that the woman was said to "roar like a blowtorch."

"From all my experience," said Coroner Beccle, "I have never come across a case so very mysterious as this."

Since the woman hadn't been smoking or come in contact with anyone holding a lit cigarette, this case appears to be yet another example of spontaneous human combustion.

Do you still have your grain of salt? It's time to swallow it.

An Attractive Suggestion?

Is SHC more likely to occur during times of increased solar magnetic activity? That's the suggestion made by Livingston Gearhart in an article he wrote for Pursuit, the journal of the Society for the Investigation of the Unexplained. Gearhart based his tentative conclusion on six alleged SHC cases, spanning some 60 years. Think about it. Six selected cases over more than half a century. Are you convinced?

A few years ago, Dutch mathematician Jan Willem Nienhuys dug through the many layers of the Phyllis Newcombe story and found the truth lying squashed at the bottom. The 22-year-old victim, it turns out, had attended a dance party at Shire Hall in Chelmsford, England, with her fiancé, Henry McAusland. The party had ended, and most of the revelers had begun to file out of the ballroom, which was on the second floor. Phyllis and Henry had lingered awhile and then made their way to the exit door.

Henry, who was in front of Phyllis, had reached the top of the staircase when he heard a shriek. Phyllis was wearing a tulle and satin dress with a very poufy skirt. When Henry turned, he saw the hem of Phyllis's dress aglow with hot, yellow flames. Panicked, Phyllis spun around and raced back into the ballroom, where she collapsed on the floor, her dress now blazing.

There were still several dozen people left in the room. They hurried to Phyllis's aid, wrapping her in coats to extinguish the flames. An ambulance had been called, and she was rushed to the hospital. She had sustained third-degree burns on her legs and torso. This is a far cry from being reduced to a pile of gray ash. Her burns were treated at the hospital, and she began to make progress. But then things took a turn for the worse when her wounds became infected—not uncommon with serious burns. She developed pneumonia and died on September 15, 1938.

Had Phyllis Newcombe spontaneously combusted? Let's put it this way. It is far more likely that a still-burning match, used to light a cigarette by someone on the staircase, had ignited her highly flammable dress.

>> Where There's Fire, There May Be a Smokescreen

But what about Mrs. Reeser and Dr. Bentley? What about the contessa?

Stage magicians will tell you that things are not always what they appear to be and that the public allows itself to be fooled. This is not to say that people are idiots or that spontaneous human combustion is a trick of some kind. But human beings love marvels and wonders and would rather embrace the highly improbable than settle for the boring old facts.

How many times do you suppose the tale of the contessa's fiery demise has been told and retold since the 1700s? Do you really believe that nothing has been added, that no bit of fiction has crept in?

Of course, there is that very disturbing photograph of John Bentley's leg. . . .

Under the right conditions, hay, oily rags, and other highly flammable materials can sometimes ignite without an external flame source. When bacteria begin to break down hay, for example, heat gradually builds up. If there is no way for the heat to escape, the temperature can climb high enough to start the hay burning. People, though, are another story.

Two hundred years ago, some people believed that the intestines produced flammable gases that could somehow erupt into flame. This is not true. Then it was theorized that a combination of alcohol and body fat could cause spontaneous combustion. But the human body is mostly salt water. Although the skin burns fairly easily, the body does not. How do we know this? People have tried it.

Not long after the Reeser case came to light, forensic anthropologist Wilton Krogman decided to conduct a little experiment. Krogman burned lots and lots of cadavers (human bodies used in research) in his lab in Pennsylvania. He built fires

Forensic anthropologist Wilton Krogman.

This photograph was taken in a laboratory where scientists tested various theories about spontaneous human combustion.

with hickory wood, coal, gasoline, and kerosene, but none of them was hot enough to incinerate a body. Only by cremating it, said Krogman, could a body be reduced to a pile of ashes. And the process of cremation uses high heat—not flames.

Krogman speculated that Mrs. Reeser had been murdered, cremated, and then spilled, if you will, onto the floor of her apartment by someone with a sick sense of staging. But since that seems almost as farfetched as the original theory, we should take another look at the scene on the evening before Mrs. Reeser's death. Woman puts on highly flammable clothes, takes sleeping pill, lights cigarette, sits down in overstuffed armchair. Fictional details will be added later.

And what about John Bentley? He was, it seems, a pipe smoker, and not a very tidy one at that. He often spilled hot ashes on himself, as evidenced by the tiny burn holes in his robes. He also kept wooden matches in his pockets. So the scene is set.

A burning ember from Dr. Bentley's pipe falls on his robe, which begins to smolder. Unable to put out what is slowly but surely becoming a little fire, Dr. Bentley gets to his feet and makes his way into the bathroom. But he is 90 and slow, and when he reaches the closest water source, he finds that the fire has really gained a foothold. Perhaps he falls. The flames advance, soon reaching the matches in his pockets. Dr. Bentley is engulfed in fire. Human combustion? Yes. Spontaneous? No.

Mary Reeser, John Bentley, and other alleged victims of SHC apparently became their own fuel source, the way the molten wax of a candle is used to keep the wick burning. Dr. Dougal Drysdale of the University of Edinburgh in Scotland says that a human body can be thought of as a candle turned inside out. Body fat corresponds to the wax, and clothing is the wick. But the body may burn like a log, with flames running along its length.

Author Larry Arnold has written a book called *Ablaze!* in which he discusses the tragic deaths of Mary Reeser, John Bentley, and other supposed SHC victims. Arnold suggests that a "subatomic pyrotron"—a wholly fictional something-or-other—is the cause of SHC.

What do you think?

CHAPTER 2
A REMEMBRANCE OF THINGS PAST

In 1952 businessman and amateur hypnotist Morey Bernstein hypnotized a woman whom he would later call Virginia Tighe. Bernstein had
Virginia recalling events so far into her past that he felt certain one more
leap would turn her into an embryo. But Virginia surprised him. She
skipped being conceived entirely and instead cut straight to her previous
life as an Irish woman named Bridey Murphy.

What?

Well, that's what Bernstein believed. The truth was something else entirely, but Bernstein wouldn't find that out until after he had made some big bucks on a book, a record, and a movie. Although many cultures have embraced the idea of reincarnation, never before had there been such undeniable proof. Here was a young Colorado housewife speaking with an authentic Irish accent and vividly describing her life in nineteenth-century Cork.

But hypnosis is a tricky business. Hypnotized subjects are very sensitive to the hypnotist's suggestions, even if they are subtle. And contrary to what many people believe, the subject is not in a "trance." Instead, he or she is simply very relaxed and, in a sense, playing a game with the hypnotist, wanting to please, anxious to create. So it doesn't take much to lead a subject along a particular path. In addition, the brain has an astonishing ability to store even the tiniest bits of data. You know things you

Facing page: This photo shows Virginia Tighe and her grandchildren. During hypnosis sessions with Morey Bernstein (*near left*), Virginia claimed to have lived a previous life as a woman named Bridey Murphy.

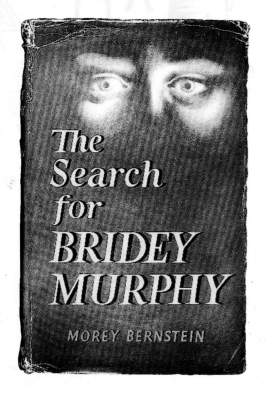

Morey Bernstein wrote *The Search for Bridey Murphy*, which describes his experience working with Virginia Tighe.

think you don't know, as was the case with Virginia Tighe.

In response to Bernstein's leading questions, Virginia fashioned a red-headed Irish persona for herself out of genuine childhood memories. Bridey's house, for example, was the spitting image of the house in which Virginia had lived when she was a child. Bridey's mother was named Kathleen, the same as Virginia's mother. Bridey said her brother had died when she was four; Virginia was five when her brother died. Virginia was active in dramatics in school and had memorized a number of Irish monologues, delivering them with a thick Irish accent. According to her uncle, Virginia sometimes danced an Irish jig on the street for passersby to earn a few pennies. Under hypnosis, she once jumped up and began to dance an Irish jig. And it goes on. A little research on Bernstein's part would have unearthed where the Bridey Murphy story came from, but as we have seen, people like fantastic stuff. Reality can be such a bore.

Virginia Tighe's past life as Bridey Murphy may have been fiction, but the belief in reincarnation—or the transmigration of souls, as it is sometimes called—is worldwide. Humans have always understood that living things die. Flowers wither. Leaves grow brittle and tumble from their branches. But other living things return. In the spring, there are buds on the trees. Green shoots pop up from the softening ground. Robins come back from their winter homes. Why can't people come back after death?

A WEIGHTY MATTER

If the soul exists, it stands to reason that it is made of something. Everything, after all, is made of something—even light. So if the soul is released at the moment of death, you would expect the body to weigh slightly less than it did before death. But experiments on animals have shown a weight gain after death. When researchers studied humans, they found that the mysterious weight gain also shows up when people are sleeping and meditating. Have they weighed the soul, or have they stumbled on something even more intriguing?

Most people feel, deeply and unshakably, that there is more to us than just atoms. Somewhere within us—although we have no idea where—there is an invisible essence, a soul, that is lasting and eternal. Our bodies will die, but our souls will not. It is this soul, the essential *us*, that allows for reincarnation. Many people believe that death releases the soul so it can move into another body. This occurs again and again, and a single soul experiences many different lives.

The Greek philosopher Plato believed that people have a vague and shadowy knowledge of these past lives. But in Greek myth, such memories were taken away. All souls had to drink from the river of forgetfulness before they could be reborn. The Jewish mystics also taught that past life memories were erased. You were struck by an angel, they said, just under your nose, and that little dent we all have is what remains of the blow. Hinduism teaches that your deeds in this life determine the form you will be given in the next one. So even if you don't retain specific memories of past lives, your donkey shape should give you certain hints.

A lot of people—both famous and not so famous—are convinced that they have been reincarnated many times. They describe, as vividly as Virginia Tighe, their lives as members of the court of King Louis XIV of France, slaves in Egypt, Civil War soldiers, Roman gladiators, and other such Hollywood extras. Hypnosis, that great fiction factory and planting field of false memories, got them in touch with their previous personalities, they say. Have they done any research to find out if these knights, dancing girls, and toga makers actually existed? No, of course not. There was no need. And, really, how can you find evidence of a grape grower who lived in Atlantis 9,000 years ago? Everybody knows Atlantis was destroyed, right?

>> An Intriguing Case

Mainstream scientists have pretty much ignored claims of reincarnation because they do not like things that can't be tested. What must be established first, they say, is proof that the soul exists, since it is the soul that presumably travels from one body to the next. Neuroscientists point out that in order for the soul to store the memories of past lives, it would have to be made of matter, like the brain. This doesn't necessarily mean the soul has to be visible to the naked eye. We can't see radioactivity, magnetism, or gravity. But we know they exist because we have instruments that can detect them. So, many scientists insist that the soul should also be detectable.

But not everyone is waiting for the soul to be found. Psychologists such as Erlendur Haraldsson, a professor from the University of Iceland, have been investigating past life claims made by very young children—those among

Erlendur Haraldsson, a psychologist who has investigated young children's stories of past lives

us who have the fewest life experiences upon which to draw. What is so astonishing about these cases is the age at which these children begin talking about their previous lives. Most mention it as soon as they have the vocabulary for it, as early as 18 months old.

Well, you may be thinking, these kids are obviously just playing. They're pretending to be grown-up, pretending to be pirates and princesses. Cartoons put these ideas into their heads.

Ah, maybe not. Let us consider the very intriguing case of a little boy named Nazih al-Danaf, who lived near Beirut, Lebanon. According to his mother, Nazih was less than two years old when he told her, "I am not small. I am big. I carry two pistols. I carry four hand grenades. Don't be scared by the hand grenades. I know how to handle them. I have a lot of weapons."

Just a little boy playing soldier? Read on.

"My children are young," said Nazih. "I want to go and see them." There were also promissory notes, he claimed, papers for money that he had lent to people. He wanted to go back to his previous village and collect the debts.

This was from a child who was not yet two years old.

Nazih's mother had her suspicions. Nazih's family are Druzes, members of an Arabic-speaking people of the Middle East. The Druze religion is related to Islam, and the concept of reincarnation is fundamental to both. Nazih's words, so inappropriate for a toddler, suggested only one thing to Nazih's mother. Her son was speaking of a past life. Without prompting, he told his family that his name had been Fuad and that he had lived in a two-story house in the village of Qaberchamoun. "It was like a villa,"

Nazih and his family are members of the Druze people, as are the men shown here.

he said, "with trees around it." He had owned a red car. "Armed people came and shot at us," he continued, and as Fuad, he had died from his wounds.

The months wore on, and Nazih became more and more insistent that he be taken back to Qaberchamoun. According to his father, he was two and a half when he drew a map of the house he had lived in as Fuad. "If you don't take me there," he said, "I am going to walk." This went on for more than three years. At last, Nazih's parents gave in. When Nazih was six, off they went to look for a family they had never met and knew nothing about.

As they drew closer to Qaberchamoun, Nazih became very animated, pointing out roads he said he remembered and supplying directions. "Take me to where I can see the white villa on the other side of the valley," Nazih told his father. "I used to see it from my house."

Fuad's wife, Najdiyah, was picking olives in the garden when her children yelled for her to come and see this little boy who was claiming to be her husband. Again, because reincarnation is fundamental to the Druze religion, nobody thought any of this was weird. But Najdiyah was not ready to believe Nazih just yet. First, she had a few test questions for him.

> "Who," she asked, "built the foundation of this gate at the entrance of this house?"
> "A man from the Faraj family," said Nazih.

One right.

> "Did I ever have an accident when we were living in our other house?"

"Yes. You fell and dislocated your shoulder."

Two right.

"How did Fairuz [their daughter] become sick?"
"She was poisoned from my medication," said Nazih, "and I took her to the hospital."

Three right.

A STRENGTH-OF-CASE SCALE

Although many societies believe in reincarnation, scientists have yet to be convinced. A few, however, are conducting serious investigation into the concept.

Researchers at the University of Virginia have been looking into possible reincarnation cases over the past 30 years. They have developed a strength-of-case scale based on 22 broad categories. These include birthmarks, wounds, and diseases shared by the subject and the person he or she claims to have been in a past life, as well as similar behaviors, such as food cravings, table manners, and skills.

Each category is assigned a number of points between −8 and +8, based on the strength of the evidence. The higher the number of points a subject scores, the stronger the case for reincarnation. Of the 799 cases in the University's database, scores ranged from a low of −3 to a high of 49 out of a possible 84 points. Conclusive? No.
Intriguing? Absolutely.

Nazih got almost everything right, in fact. He knew where Fuad had kept his guns and the kind of the pistol he had given his brother as a gift. He knew where the barrel was where Fuad had taught Najdiyah to shoot. Yes, the family had owned a red car. Yes, he knew that upon two occasions, Israeli soldiers had jump-started their car when it had broken down on the way back from Beirut. He correctly identified pictures of Fuad's father and brothers. And yes, Fuad had died just the way Nazih had said.

Erlendur Haraldsson visited Lebanon six times, from 1988 to 2001, to interview all the people involved with this case. He found that of the 23 statements Nazih made about his past life as Fuad, 17 turned out to be correct and 5 could not be checked. Haraldsson dismisses the suggestion that everyone was lying, hoaxing, or conspiring to put one over on him. All the stories were consistent over time, and nobody stood to gain anything by talking with Haraldsson. So we are left with . . . what?

Both families are convinced that Fuad was reborn as Nazih nine years after his death. Haraldsson does not say what he thinks. But it is interesting to note that when children start speaking about having been someone else, they do so almost as soon as they develop the ability to form words. Most are very insistent and continue to talk about a past life until they are about eight years old. And then, for whatever reason, they stop. Is that because the memories have faded away?

Science cannot explain everything. Perhaps one day it will catch up with religious belief. But perhaps it is not meant to.

CHAPTER 3
THE GHOST WORE A DRESS

26

Everybody loves a good ghost story, and many of us have one or two to tell. Take, for example, Mary Zeremenko of Pittsburgh, Pennsylvania. She had never believed in ghosts, she said, assuming that all the funny sounds in her 80-year-old house were being made by squirrels or settling floors. She didn't even raise an eyebrow when her 2-year-old daughter Alexandra began talking about the "people in the living room." Most children have imaginary friends, right?

Sometimes Mary would hear Alexandra cautioning people not to sit on the sofa, an antique the family had purchased at an estate sale. "No, no!" Alexandra often cried out when a visitor eyed the graceful Victorian. "There are people already there!" And again, Mary didn't think much of it. But when Max, Alexandra's little brother, started saying good morning to the living room people and asking how they were, Mary decided that things were starting to get a little weird.

The invisible people in the living room continued to interact with Mary's children without incident until one day, about a year later, when Max burst into the kitchen. "People hit Max!" he shouted, tears streaming down his cheeks. He led Mary into the living room and showed her a glass lamp teetering on the edge of a small table. Max had been tugging on the doily upon which the lamp stood, and one more inch would

Mary Zeremenko's children, Max (*left*) and Alexandra (*right*), sit on the family's haunted sofa. As teenagers, they no longer see the "living room people."

have spelled disaster. But a ghostly slap on the wrist had supposedly stopped Max and saved the lamp.

After that little episode, Mary called in a psychic who said, yes, indeed, there were ghosts in the house, but they were only in the living room. They had apparently moved in with the sofa. Sometimes, said the psychic, people become overly attached to their possessions and refuse to give them up, even after they die. In this case, the previous owners had been two unmarried sisters who, instead of passing into the next world, decided to stay here with their beloved couch.

Mary's children don't see the ghosts anymore, having outgrown them, perhaps. Mary's never seen them, but she says they're welcome to stay. Her husband thinks everybody is crazy—except, maybe, the psychic, who made sure he handed Mary a bill for his services, whatever those might have been.

>> Services Rendered?

As a rule, psychics don't do very much. They take "readings" of the room and "sense" make-believe things such as inverted force fields and negative energy—indications, they say, of the presence of spirits. But because our belief in ghosts is so strong, we make few demands for real proof. A psychic only has to say, "Oooo. Here's a cold spot. Do you feel it? Stand next to me. Feel it? I'll bet you do." And the person—who already believes there's a ghost somewhere, or why call in a psychic?—says, "Yes! Yes! I do!" The psychic then pronounces the room haunted, and everyone's happy. But rooms, especially rooms in old houses, don't heat evenly. Some spots are naturally cooler than others—next to a fireplace, for example, if the flue has been left open. People rarely pay much attention to these little temperature differences, but when you're hunting ghosts, the less that is explained, the better. And the human imagination is the psychic's most trusted assistant.

But why are people so willing, so downright anxious, to believe in ghosts? Many of us claim to have heard them, felt them, and actually seen them. But if we were interviewed, would we pay attention to our own rather hard-to-believe description?

—What do they look like? we might be asked.

—Whitish stuff, kind of wispy. You can see through them. Smoky, sort of. Light, very light.

—Do they look like people?

—Oh, yes. I once saw the little girl who haunts the old Ebbington Inn. She was dressed in a lovely pinafore. I didn't see the man who murdered her, but I did hear his footsteps.

—This light, airy entity makes noise when it walks?

—Certainly. And sometimes he opens the windows on the top floor.

Well, now, come on. Does any of this make sense to you? But the concept of the ghost is very ancient and an important part of many belief

This photograph, taken in 1891, shows the ghost of Combermere Abbey in Cheshire, England . . . or does it? Note the figure that seems to be seated in the chair at the left.

The Convicts Go A'Haunting

The Hyde Park Barracks is reported to be the "most haunted building in Central Sydney," Australia. Built in the early 1800s, it housed about 600 male convicts who slept in 12 rooms slung with hammocks. Today it is a museum, but just for fun, sometimes the barracks opens its doors for ghostly sleepovers. Spooky encounters have included footsteps, the sighting of a man in period clothing, and "chilling sensations" on the third floor.

systems. Some cultures look favorably upon ghosts, whereas others take elaborate steps to prevent a person's ghost from coming back to haunt the living. There are good ghosts and bad ghosts—ghosts who are pains in the neck, and ghosts who are funny and playful. Their favorite hangouts are graveyards (naturally), castles, ships, quaint inns, and places where people died violent deaths. And ghosts are big business. They are used to lure guests to old hotels where an overnight stay (or two or three) could result in a deliciously spooky midnight sighting. Ghosts bring tourists to battlefields they might not otherwise have considered visiting. But most of all, ghosts are the psychic's meat and potatoes. Without ghosts, most psychics would have to admit they were in show business.

The team that started the spiritualism craze was the Fox sisters—Catherine, Leah, and Margaret. In 1848 these precocious teens from Hydesville, New York, announced that they had begun to hear mysterious rapping sounds in their bedroom. One night the knocking was so loud that the entire family was roused from bed and forced to leave the house. Not long after that, the girls took their act on the road and started calling up ghostly rappings for the general public. People flocked to the Fox sisters' séances, held hands and closed their eyes, and fully believed they were getting messages from their dearly departed. But alas, it was only the sisters' toe joints, cracking away within the girls' shoes, that spoke to the hoodwinked customers.

As spiritualism began to catch on, mediums and psychics became pretty good at contacting dead Uncle Charlie. Séance rooms were abuzz with levitating tables, tooting

The Fox sisters *(seated)* levitate a table during a séance in 1850.

trumpets that hovered above people's heads, tinny-sounding voices from beyond the grave, and whatever else the psychics could dream up to out-spook their competitors. And the public ate it up. Even when dozens of mediums were unmasked as frauds, people continued to slap down money for a chance to chat with Napoleon's mother-in-law. Ghosts exist, they had long ago decided, and that was that.

Ask around and in no time at all, you're bound to come across someone who thinks he or she has seen a ghost. That, at least, is the assumption, because what else could the apparition have been? Without knowing there are other possibilities,

33

people often leap to the rather preposterous conclusion that they saw the disembodied spirit of a dead person. Well, say the ghostbusters, not so fast.

>> Things that Go Bump in the Night

In his many years with the Committee for the Scientific Investigation of Claims of the Paranormal (CSICOP), investigator Joe Nickell has slept in a lot of haunted inns. Once a place gets the reputation for being haunted, he says, people expect to see ghosts. Their imagination is fired up even before they walk through the door. Add to this the appropriate decor—heavy draperies, perhaps, or a great ticking clock—and not to see a ghost would be downright embarrassing. Sometimes innkeepers invent ghost stories as a way of drawing in the clientele. And

Investigator Joe Nickell has spent many years chasing down ghosts.

A blurry figure appears in the center of this photo taken in the cellars of the Viaduct Inn in London, England, which were once the cells of Newgate Prison. The photographer claims no one was in front of him when he photographed the empty cell.

then, to keep the game going, they "stage" a little ghostly activity. Hey, if the mediums can do it, why not a hotel owner with a magician's manual?

Ghosts seem to have a tendency to appear after everyone has gone to sleep. Even in the movies, they have a particular fondness for popping up at the foot of the bed. Rarely, if ever, does a ghost sit down at the breakfast table and help himself to your ham and eggs. Nickell and others believe it's because a lot of ghosts are actually hypnagogic hallucinations.

A hypnagogic hallucination is a dream of sorts, but it occurs just as we are drifting off to sleep. Our brainwaves

Did Abraham Lincoln See a Ghost?

"It was just after my election in 1860," Lincoln told his friend, Noah Brooks. "I was well tired out, and went home to rest. . . . Opposite where I lay was a bureau, with a swinging glass [mirror] upon it, and looking in that glass, I saw myself reflected. . . . But my face, I noticed, had two separate and distinct images. I was a little bothered, perhaps startled, and got up and looked in the glass, but the illusion vanished.

"On lying down again I saw it a second time—plainer, if possible, than before. And then I noticed that one of the faces was a little paler . . . than the other. I got up and the thing melted away. . . . I went off, and in the excitement of the hour, forgot all about it—nearly, but not quite, for the thing would once in a while come up, and give me a little pang, as though something uncomfortable had happened.

" . . . [A] few days after I tried the experiment again, when, sure enough, the thing came again; but I never succeeded in bringing the ghost back after that."

show a distinct pattern that is unlike either wakefulness or sleep. We are on the outer edge of both, which is why the strange sounds and fanciful images seem so real. We think that our eyes are open, that we are sitting up in bed, peering through the darkness at silhouetted, shadowy people. Add to this an earlier suggestion by your friendly chambermaid that your room may be haunted, and a hypnagogic hallucination can become a ghost sighting.

And there's another trick our brain likes to play on us. It's called a waking dream, or reverie. The word *reverie* comes from the French and means "to wander" or "to be delirious." Again, it is late at night. The hotel lobby is empty, and the guests are safely tucked in their rooms. The night clerk sits on a stool behind the front desk, idly turning the pages of a newspaper he has already read. He is bored, and his mind is drifting. Suddenly, from the corner of his eye, he glimpses the figure of a woman. He looks up, and she vanishes.

A photographer in Wem, England, shot this photograph of a fire at Wem Town Hall in November 1995. A girl the photographer had not seen mysteriously appeared in the photograph. Local legend tells of a 14-year-old girl who dropped a candle and started a fire that burned the entire town to the ground in 1677.

But she is not a ghost. She is, instead, a reverie, a mental image stored in the night clerk's brain from another place and time. In the silence of the hotel lobby, the visual memory pops up, and then, in a blink, it is gone.

Psychologist Michael Persinger has shown that sometimes a simple magnetic field can trigger a ghostly apparition. The eye is actually an extension of the brain. It collects information and sends it to three areas, called lobes, in the part of the brain called the cerebrum. That's where the brain interprets the data and turns it into images. One of these areas, the temporal lobe, plays a role in storing the images. In some people, the

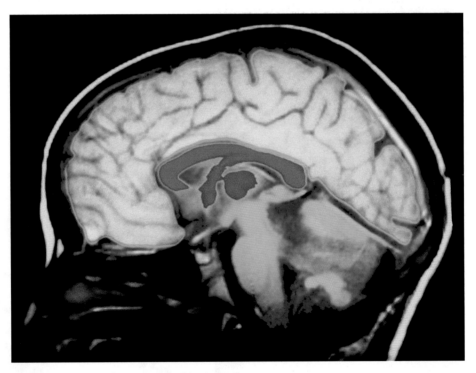

This image of a human brain was taken using magnetic resonance imagery (MRI) technology. Scientists are exploring brain activity to see if it plays a role in seeing ghostly apparitions.

temporal lobe is very sensitive. Persinger found that when these people were exposed to a magnetic field, it triggered a ghostly sighting. And they didn't have to stand next to an electro-magnet for it to happen. Computers, TVs, and even clock radios create magnetic fields. So for some of us, seeing a ghost may be as easy as hitting the snooze button.

It is not the job of the skeptics to prove that ghosts don't exist. It's up to the ghostly investigators to prove that they do. Ghost stories and legends are not enough. Photos people claim to have taken of ghosts are suspect. And the human brain likes to play tricks. Why else would so many ghosts be wearing such lovely dresses?

Near-Death
Experiences

A critically ill woman is wheeled into the emergency room, her blood pressure perilously low. Seconds later, she goes into cardiac arrest. "Code Blue!" shouts one of the nurses, and suddenly everyone is on the move. The woman hears the words and decides she is in trouble. But she feels detached and strangely at peace. She senses movement and realizes she has left her body. She is floating inches from the ceiling, watching the doctors and nurses desperately trying to save her life. There is a loud thud as the crash cart paddles deliver an electrical shock to her heart. "Clear!" yells one of the doctors, and she is given another shock. She watches her body jump. She is fascinated by the proceedings.

The woman begins to pull away from the scene and feels as if she is moving through a tunnel. There is light all around her, a brilliant white light that enfolds her with its warmth. She is calm and serene, comforted by the heavenly radiance of the light. She sees her older brother, who had died years before in a car crash. He is smiling. Far in the distance, at the end of the tunnel, an indistinct being stands silhouetted against the blinding light. The woman has a wonderful sense of who the being is, and a flood of deep peace washes over her. She wants nothing but to remain here in this place of love and light, but the being tells her she must go back. It is not her time. "No!" she begs. "Please let me stay!" But the being is insistent. Go back . . . go back . . . go back . . . go back. . . .

"I've got a pulse! Pressure's coming up."

The woman's heart gains strength.

"One hundred over sixty. We're looking good."

"Welcome home, honey," says one of the nurses. But welcome home from where?

>> All in the Mind?

A 1982 Gallup poll found that 5 percent of the population had had a similar experience when they came close to dying. All felt themselves separate from their body and then move through a tunnel or spiral toward a brilliant light. All felt an overwhelming sense of peace and oneness and "returned" with the unshakable belief that death is not the end. And all said they were no longer afraid of dying. They knew what awaited them, and it was beautiful beyond description.

This photograph is a double exposure taken to represent an out-of-body experience.

Well, you can just imagine what the starched shirt medical community thought of all this. They rolled their eyes, made a few faces, and dismissed the whole thing with a unified flick of the wrist. "These people," they said, "are either exaggerating or have a very overactive imagination. A journey into the next world? We think not." But the reports would not go away. In fact, their numbers increased as more and more patients came forward with astonishing—and strikingly similar—tales of their near-death experience (NDE).

Psychologists, as you might expect, were the first to become interested in the NDE phenomenon. Why, they wondered, was everybody seeing basically the same thing? If this were simply wishful thinking about the hereafter, wouldn't people fashion heaven to suit their personal tastes? Wouldn't children, who were also reporting NDEs, imagine a vast amusement park, for instance, or a play-ground, or even a toy store? Lights and tunnels are such unlikely choices for kids.

Then there were the out-of-body experiences. Accident victims who had no vital signs, who had been unconscious and inches from death, later described in detail the crash scene, the paramedics' rescue efforts, and the ambulance. Cardiac patients knew what the emergency room doctors had done to resuscitate them. Some people even said they had seen the nurses' ID badges clearly enough to read the names. How could this be? Had these people actually left their bodies? Even the re-searchers—many of whom were doctors—began to wonder.

Accident victims may later be able to provide detailed descriptions of how they were rescued, even if they were unconscious at the time.

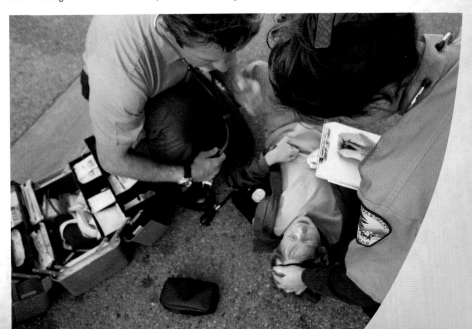

But as it turns out, the out-of-body experience is not unique to the NDE. Certain drugs, such as Ketamine, will bring on the same sensation, creating the illusion that you have left your body and are floating around somewhere high above. These drugs block the brain receptors for a substance called glutamate. A flood of glutamate is released when blood flow, oxygen, and blood sugar levels drop—the kinds of things that occur in the body of a person who is in critical condition. But too much glutamate will kill brain cells, so the body apparently responds by triggering a substance that blocks the glutamate. First, last, and always, the brain protects itself.

But how, you are probably going to ask, were these people able to describe what was going on around them? How did they know what was

Many survivors of near-death experiences report having seen a tunnel of light.

happening? They were unconscious. They couldn't see anything. Ah, but they could still hear. This particular sense, for whatever reason, continues to function when the other four have been stilled. It may not be perfect, but it works well enough to deliver information about an environment the person can no longer interact with. We also have countless images stored in our brain. Hearing the jolt from a crash cart would call up the pictures we have seen of people being resuscitated—if not actually, then on TV. Our visual filing system is immense. Because our brain continually tries to make sense of what is happening to us, it will do whatever is necessary to fill in the gaps. So the out-of-body experience is really just an illusion, a movie that is written and directed by our astonishing brain.

What about the tunnel and the light? Well, it seems they're also hallucinations, brought on by a lack of oxygen to the brain.

Finally, people probably have similar NDEs because we all have similar wiring. We are individual and unique in countless ways, but our physiology is the same. The variations in our chemistries are minor and unimportant. We share the body human and because of that, we react as one as we approach the big sleep.

If NDEs are not a glimpse into a heavenly hereafter, they are still an extraordinary phenomenon. They show us that as we drift out of this world, our genius brain bathes us in light and comforts us with natural brain chemicals. We will not, as the poet Dylan Thomas wrote, "rage, rage against the dying of the light," but slip softly into the arms of eternity. And that might, indeed, be our heaven.

>> Find Out More

Books// Blackwood, Gary L. *Long-Ago Lives.* New York: Benchmark Books, 1999.
This book examines case studies of reincarnation, including the use of hypnosis to try to find out about past lives.

Cohen, Daniel and Susan. *Hauntings and Horrors: The Ultimate Guide to Spooky America.* New York: Dutton Children's Books, 2002.
This guide to creepy places across the United States includes a variety of sites that are said to be haunted. Travel directions and telephone numbers are provided so you can visit these places and decide for yourself whether they're really haunted.

Landau, Elaine. *Near-Death Experiences.* Brookfield, CT: Millbrook Press, 1996.
This book describes the various kinds of near-death experiences and explains how scientists study NDE cases.

Videos// *Ghostbusters.* Prod. and dir. Ivan Reitman; writ. Dan Aykroyd and Harold Ramis. Culver City, CA: Columbia TriStar Home Video, 1999. Videocassette.
In this hilarious take on hauntings, three unemployed parapsychology professors set up shop as a ghost removal service.

Prophetic Voices: Personal Accounts of Near-Death Experiences. Narr: Kenneth Ring. Sunnyvale, CA: Video Sig, 1981.
In this documentary produced by public TV station WGBY, four people give detailed accounts of their near-death experiences.

Websites// *The Skeptiseum: Ghosts and Spirits*
<http://www.skeptiseum.org/exhibits/ghostsspirits/index.html>
The Skeptiseum is a virtual museum of artifacts related to paranormal topics. This wing contains a variety of exhibits including a spirit trumpet used in seances and photographs supposedly containing images of ghosts.

Spontaneous Human Combustion
<http://anomalyinfo.com/shc/index.htm>
This website gives a broad overview of spontaneous human combustion, including the history of SHC, descriptions of many cases, and a variety of SHC theories.

47

>> About the Author

Born in Baltimore, Maryland, Judith Herbst grew up in Queens, New York, where she learned to jump double Dutch with amazing skill. She has since lost that ability. A former English teacher, she ran away from school in her tenure year to become a writer. Her first book for kids was *Sky Above and Worlds Beyond,* whose title, she admits, was much too long. She loves to write and would rather be published, she says, than be rich, which has turned out to be the case. Herbst spends summers in Maine on a lake with her cats and laptop.

>> Photo Acknowledgments

Photographs and illustrations in this book are used with the permission of: Fortean Picture Library, pp. 6, 7, 8, 14, 18, 30, 32, 35, 44; Larry E. Arnold/Fortean Picture Library, p. 9; From the Collections of the University of Pennsylvania Archives, p. 13; © Bettmann/CORBIS, pp. 16, 17; Guy Lyon Playfair/Fortean Picture Library, p. 21; © Hanan Isachar/CORBIS, p. 22; ©Pittsburgh Post-Gazette, 2004, all rights reserved. Reprinted with permission, p. 27; © Hulton-Deutsch Collection/CORBIS, p. 33; The Skeptical Inquirer Magazine, p. 34; Tony O'Rahilly/Fortean Picture Library, p. 37; © Royalty-Free/CORBIS, p. 38; Philip Panton/Fortean Picture Library, p. 42; © Ronnie Kaufman/CORBIS, p. 43. Illustrations by Bill Hauser, pp. 4–5, 10, 26, 29, 40.

Cover image by © Brian Cencula/CORBIS.